ELEANOR ROOSEVELT

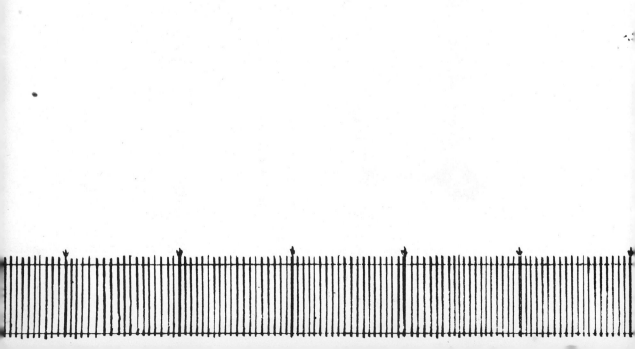

A CROWELL BIOGRAPHY
ELEANOR ROOSEVELT

By Jane Goodsell

Illustrated by Wendell Minor

THOMAS Y. CROWELL COMPANY   NEW YORK

CROWELL BIOGRAPHIES · *Edited by Susan Bartlett Weber*

COPYRIGHT © 1970 BY JANE GOODSELL

ILLUSTRATIONS COPYRIGHT © 1970 BY WENDELL MINOR

MANUFACTURED IN THE UNITED STATES OF AMERICA

Published in Canada by Fitzhenry & Whiteside Limited, Toronto

L. C. Card 71-106573

ISBN 0-690-25626-4 (LB)

3   4   5   6   7   8   9   10

ELEANOR ROOSEVELT

A CROWELL
BIOGRAPHY

The tall brown house in New York City was quiet. The little girl was almost asleep. Suddenly, she woke with a start. Someone was calling her name.

"Eleanor!" It was her aunt calling from across the hall. "My throat is sore and I have no ice! Would you bring me some from the icebox, please?"

Eleanor caught her breath. The icebox was outside the basement door. It was late at night, and she was afraid of the dark.

She tiptoed down the stairs of the big, gloomy

house. She felt her way through the black basement. Her heart beat so fast that she could hardly breathe. But she returned upstairs with the ice.

Her aunt thanked her, and told her she was a good girl. Eleanor only smiled, but she felt warm and happy inside. She was not praised often. People were more likely to scold her. "Eleanor, stand up straight!" "Take your thumb out of your mouth, Eleanor!"

The little girl was very shy, and she seldom smiled. She wished that she could be gay and laugh easily. She longed to be like her mother, who had died when Eleanor was eight. But her mother had been beautiful, and Eleanor knew that she did not look like her mother. She had a solemn face and straight blond hair. Her mother had often called her a plain and awkward child.

Eleanor had no friends her own age to play with. She spent long hours thinking about her father. She knew that he was dead, but he was

still with her in her daydreams. Her father was the only person who had ever made Eleanor feel loved.

Someday, this shy and lonely little girl would have friends all over the world. She would grow up to become the wife of the President of the United States. Her name, Eleanor Roosevelt, would be known to people everywhere.

Now she was ten years old, and she was an orphan. She lived in her grandmother's house in New York City. Her four-year-old brother, Hall, lived there, too. So did two of her aunts and two uncles.

The rooms were dim and shadowy at night in the light of the gas lamps. Houses did not have electric lights in 1894. There were no cars then, either. Carriages drawn by horses clattered past the house.

Summers, the family moved to Tivoli on the Hudson River. Eleanor's grandmother had a large country house there. Sometimes Eleanor and her little brother went on picnics with their aunts and uncles. Sometimes they played hide-and-seek. Still, Eleanor spent a great deal of time by herself.

Eleanor's grandmother did not think children needed playmates. Eleanor spent most of her day

at lessons in French, music, and sewing. She was not allowed to go outside the house by herself, and she had to take a cold bath every morning. If she was naughty, she was sent to bed without supper. Even in summer she had to wear long black stockings. When it was very hot, Eleanor sometimes rolled her stockings to her ankles. But she was quickly told to pull them up. "Ladies do not show their legs!" her grandmother told her.

Eleanor's grandmother did not make these rules to be unkind. She thought it was the right way to raise children.

As Eleanor grew older, she began to go to parties and dances. Her shyness kept her from making friends easily. Often she sat by herself, wishing she were at home reading a book.

But one party was different. A tall and handsome young man asked her to dance. His name was Franklin Roosevelt. He was a distant cousin of Eleanor's.

Franklin danced several dances with Eleanor that night. He was so friendly that she did not feel shy. She talked about books she had read and places she had been.

Eleanor and Franklin did not meet again for several years. When Eleanor was fifteen years old, she was sent to a school for girls in England.

The English school had strict rules. Beds were made neatly, and drawers kept in perfect order. Every morning Eleanor had to play the piano for

an hour before breakfast. She had to study hard. Yet the three years Eleanor spent at the school were the happiest she had known. For the first time she had friends her own age.

The headmistress was very kind to Eleanor. She tried to help her get over her shyness. She taught Eleanor to choose clothes that made her look prettier. She talked to her about books and ideas. Eleanor knew that the headmistress liked her. This made her like herself better.

It was a sad day when Eleanor left England to return to her grandmother's house in New York. She dreaded what was ahead. Eleanor was now eighteen years old. At eighteen, the girls in her family entered "society." Almost every evening they went to dances and parties.

Even in her pretty new dresses Eleanor did not have a good time at dances. Once again she felt shy and lonely. She was bored, too. So many parties seemed silly to Eleanor. She wanted to do something to help other people.

She began to teach dancing and gym to little girls who lived in a slum neighborhood. There was not much fun in these children's lives. But they were gay and giggly as they twirled on their toes in Eleanor's ballet class.

One day Franklin Roosevelt came to the dance class to call for Eleanor. They had now become good friends. The little girls at the class whispered to Eleanor, "Is he your boyfriend?"

She blushed and said, "Certainly not." But the girls had guessed the truth. Franklin was falling in love with Eleanor.

He asked her to marry him, and she said yes.

Franklin's mother, Sara Roosevelt, thought they were too young to marry. She tried to get Franklin to change his mind. But Franklin was very sure that he wanted to marry Eleanor.

Their wedding took place when Eleanor was twenty-one years old. After a trip to Europe they lived in New York City, where Franklin was going to school. He was studying to become a lawyer.

Franklin's mother wanted to live near her son. She built two houses next door to each other. She lived in one herself. The other she gave to Franklin and Eleanor.

During the next few years Sara Roosevelt managed Eleanor's home. Eleanor did not know how to plan meals and give orders to servants.

Franklin's mother did not help her to learn. Sara Roosevelt wanted to run her son's home herself. She liked being the head of the family.

Eleanor's first child was a little girl. She was named Anna. A boy, James, was born a year later. Franklin's mother hired nurses to take care of the children.

Then Franklin became interested in politics. He was elected to the state Senate. The Senate held its meetings in Albany, the capital of New York State. He and his family moved to Albany.

Now Eleanor was living many miles from Franklin's mother. She had to learn how to run her own home. Eleanor learned then that she could do what had to be done. This was to be true all the rest of her life.

After three years in Albany the family moved to Washington, D.C. Franklin had an important job there, working for the Navy. Eleanor and Franklin were invited to many parties. They gave parties in their own home, too. Once it would have been very hard for Eleanor to talk to people she did not know. Now she found that she could overcome her shyness.

Her family grew. By the time Anna was ten, she had four brothers: James, who was called Jimmy; Elliott; Franklin Junior, named after his father; and John, the baby of the family.

Anna was a quiet and pretty girl with long blond hair. The boys were noisy and full of mischief. Eleanor did not raise her children by the strict rules of her own childhood. The children called their parents Mom and Pop, and they were seldom punished. Eleanor and Franklin helped with homework. The family played games together. Summers were spent at Campobello, a small island off the coast of Maine. There the children had ponies to ride. The family went on picnics and sailed boats on the bay.

At Campobello something happened that changed everything. Franklin had spent the day sailing. When he came home, he felt sick and went to bed. The next morning he had a high fever. Three days later he could not move his legs. Franklin had polio.

For several weeks no one knew whether Franklin would live or die. At last the doctors said that he was out of danger. He would live, but the illness had left his legs very weak. He would have to wear heavy leg braces for the rest of his life. He would never again walk without help.

Yet Franklin made up his mind that he would not spend his life in a wheelchair. His legs were useless, but he could move his arms and shoulders. Each day he exercised to make them stronger. He crawled on the floor. He pulled himself upstairs with his arms.

It almost broke Eleanor's heart to watch him. Yet she knew that she must not show how she felt. She must be calm and cheerful.

As Franklin grew better, he talked about the years ahead. What was he going to do with the rest of his life? Eleanor knew then that she must help him in another way. She must make sure that Franklin would someday go back to politics. It was the most important and exciting part of his life.

Franklin's mother did not agree. She had never wanted Franklin to be in politics. Now that he was crippled, she thought he should live a quiet life. She wanted him to live in her big country home at Hyde Park.

Sara Roosevelt was a very positive person. Eleanor had always been a little afraid of her. But this time Eleanor was sure that she was wrong. Franklin would not be happy unless he could take part in politics again.

First he must learn to walk with canes and crutches. Until he learned, Eleanor decided, she must keep the Roosevelt name from being forgotten.

Fighting her shyness, she made her first political speech. Her voice shook and she giggled nervously. Her second speech was a little easier. Before long she was making speeches around the state. In time she got over her fears. She learned to speak simply and naturally.

She learned to do other things she had been too timid to try before. She took swimming lessons, and learned to drive a car. She went camping with her sons, and learned to pitch a tent and paddle a canoe. Before, it had been

Franklin who did these things with his children.
Now Eleanor felt that she must take his place as
best she could.

Slowly Franklin grew stronger. At last he felt
ready to walk with crutches in public. He an-
nounced that he would make a speech at the
Democratic Convention in New York City. He
would do it to help a good friend, Alfred E.
Smith. Franklin would say that Al Smith should

be nominated for President of the United States.

It was very hot in the huge hall the night Franklin made his speech. Eleanor held her breath as he made his way slowly to the speaker's stand. His seventeen-year-old son, Jimmy, walked beside him and held his arm.

The hall was very quiet until Franklin was safely on the platform. Then the crowd stood and cheered him for his courage. Eleanor blinked back tears of pride. She knew better than anyone else how much courage it had taken.

Franklin made a strong and stirring speech about his friend. When he finished, the audience cheered and clapped for a long time. Franklin's speech did not get his friend nominated. Another man was chosen instead. But the speech Franklin made became famous. Newspapers praised his courage and his honesty. Some said that Franklin Roosevelt would be President someday.

A few years later, Franklin was elected gover-

nor of the state of New York. The Roosevelts moved once again to Albany. This time they lived in the big mansion that was the home of the governor.

Their children were growing up. Anna was married, and had children of her own. The boys were away at school.

With her children gone, Eleanor had time to help Franklin in an important way. Where he could not go on his crutches, she went in his place. She visited schools and hospitals and prisons. She learned to look at things carefully and to ask questions. Sometimes she saw that buildings were not kept clean. Sometimes she learned that people were not getting good food or were not well treated. She would tell Franklin what she had seen and heard. Then he would work to make things better.

Franklin was a very good governor. His name became known all over the country. Many people

said that he should become the next President.

Eleanor was not sure she wanted to be the wife of the President of the United States. It sounded frightening to her. She liked to dress simply, and to say what she thought. The First Lady was expected to be formal and dignified. She had to be careful to say the right things.

Eleanor worried about Franklin, too. She knew that the next President would have many problems. The United States was in trouble. Millions of people were out of work and could not find jobs. Many families had no money at all. Their children were going to bed hungry.

Yet Eleanor kept her thoughts to herself. She felt that Franklin should do what seemed best to him.

When Franklin decided to run for President, she helped him every way she could. On election night he won a great victory. He was elected President of the United States.

Eleanor turned out to be a very unusual First
Lady. She surprised the White House servants by
running the elevator herself. She often walked
instead of riding in the Presidential car. She went
into the kitchen to scramble eggs for the family.
First Ladies usually did not do such things.

She tried her best to make the White House a
homelike place to live. She brought in com-
fortable chairs and sofas. She put a swing on the
White House lawn for her grandchildren.

Eleanor shook hands with long lines of guests, as she was expected to do. But other things that she did surprised people. She went into dark coal mines to talk to miners. She served soup to hungry men who were out of work. She visited farm families living in shacks, and city families in dreary slums. Wherever there were people who needed help, Eleanor Roosevelt went to see what could be done.

All sorts of people were asked to parties at the

White House. She invited schoolchildren, college students, factory workers, farmers, and fishermen. Of course, many famous people came to the White House, too. Eleanor Roosevelt greeted everyone with the same friendly smile.

When the king and queen of England came to the United States, she gave a picnic for them at Franklin's country home at Hyde Park. She served the king and queen hot dogs and potato chips. She wanted them to know what a real American picnic was like.

Eleanor Roosevelt could never bear to see anyone treated unfairly. Once, a women's club refused to let a famous singer, Marian Anderson, sing in its Washington hall. The club did not want her because she was a Negro. Eleanor Roosevelt invited Marian Anderson to sing at the White House. She wanted the world to know that Americans were proud of Marian Anderson.

During the Second World War American

soldiers were sent to many parts of the world. Eleanor Roosevelt traveled thousands of miles to visit them. She made trips to England and to the South Pacific. She went to cheer the boys who were far from home and lonely.

Eleanor Roosevelt was loved and admired by millions of people. But she was criticized, too. Some people felt that she should be more dignified. They said she had no business flying all over the world. They called her a busybody. They told jokes about her.

She knew what they said, but she had learned that she must do what seemed right to her.

Eleanor Roosevelt lived in the White House twelve years. Franklin was elected President four times. The American people trusted him. They wanted to keep him as their leader. But the long war years were hard on Franklin. Eleanor worried about his health. He was very thin, and she knew that he was terribly tired.

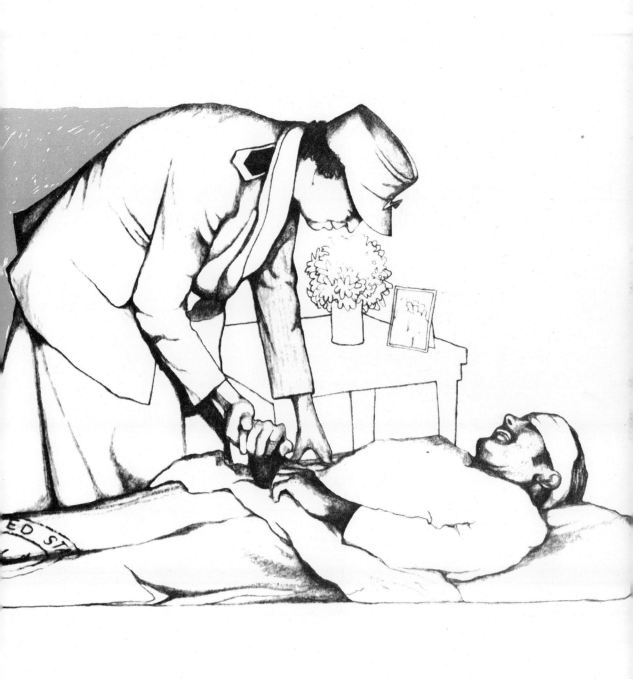

A few months after he began his fourth term as President, Franklin Roosevelt died. His sudden death shocked the world. Eleanor felt lost inside, but she kept her tears to herself. It was she who comforted others. Her strength helped them to be strong, too.

Now Eleanor was no longer the First Lady. She left the White House for Hyde Park. She

moved into a small cottage because the big house was too large for her now. She wanted to live simply. Most of all, she wanted to be busy and useful.

The war had ended. The United States was on the winning side. But thousands of American boys had been killed. War is sad for winners as well as losers.

The United Nations was begun in the hope of keeping peace in the world. Its first meeting was held in London in 1946. People from many countries met there.

Eleanor Roosevelt sailed for London as a member of the United States team. She served in the United Nations for six years. She worked for justice and freedom for people everywhere. She helped to write an important paper called the Declaration of Human Rights.

When her job ended in 1952, the United Nations had its own building in New York City.

Eleanor Roosevelt was now a great-grandmother. Her hair was almost white, but she did not seem old. She stayed young because she kept on growing and learning all her life.

She traveled far and wide. She went to India, Russia, Greece, Turkey, Japan, and many other countries. She spoke for the United Nations. She said it was the world's best hope for peace.

Wherever she went, she met old friends and made new ones. She had become the most famous woman in the world. People felt that she was their friend. Sometimes they threw their arms around her and hugged her. She explained very simply the love people felt for her. She said, "When you get to be my age, you are everybody's grandmother."

Visitors streamed to the little house in Hyde Park to see her. She welcomed kings and queens, presidents and prime ministers, schoolchildren and neighbors. She liked best of all the times when her own family gathered for birthdays and holidays. She loved to read fairy tales to her grandchildren and great-grandchildren.

She was seventy-eight years old when she died. Millions of people all over the world wept at the news of her death. The little girl who had no friends had grown up to be known and loved by people everywhere.

About the Author

Jane Goodsell, the author of ELEANOR ROOSEVELT, was born in Portland, Oregon, and has lived most of her life there. She has written books and magazine articles for both children and adults. She is married, and the mother of three daughters.

Mrs. Roosevelt, who had long been one of Jane Goodsell's heroines, often visited Portland when she had a granddaughter going to school there at Reed College. Once Mrs. Goodsell was lucky enough to meet Eleanor Roosevelt at a party. "She was as natural and wonderful as I expected her to be," Jane Goodsell says.

About the Illustrator

Wendell Minor studied commercial design and illustration at the Ringling School of Art in Sarasota, Florida, and at the Kansas City Art Institute. While at the Ringling School, he received Gold Awards for his work.

Since graduation Mr. Minor has designed books and book jackets as well as doing free-lance illustration.

In order to familiarize himself with Eleanor Roosevelt and her world, Wendell Minor visited Hyde Park, the Roosevelt home in New York, and did special research at the library there.